D0929106

How I Escaped From the Labyrinth
and Other Poems

PHILIP DACEY

HOW I ESCAPED
FROM THE LABYRINTH

AND OTHER POEMS

Carnegie-Mellon University Press
Pittsburgh & London 1977

For my Mother and Father
and in Memory of Dennis McGinn, 1947-1969

ACKNOWLEDGMENTS

The poems in this book have appeared previously, sometimes in another form, in the following periodicals, anthologies, and chapbooks: *American Review*; *American Poetry Anthology* (Avon); *Ardis Anthology of New American Poetry* (Ardis); *The Beast With Two Backs* (Gunrunner Press); *Beloit Poetry Journal*; *The Best of Nimrod*; *"But Is It Poetry?": An Anthology of One-Line Poems* (Dragonfly); *California Quarterly*; *Cardinal Poetry Quarterly*; *Carolina Quarterly*; *A Celebration of Cats* (Eriksson); *Centennial Review*; *College English*; *Counter/Measures*; *Denver Quarterly*; *Dragonfly*; *Esquire*; *Fish, Sweet Giraffe, the Lion, Snake and Owl* (Back Door Press); *The Gathering* (Iowa City); *Heartland II: Poets of the Midwest* (Northern Ill. U.); *International Cat Fancy*; *Ironwood*; *Just What the Country Needs, Another Poetry Anthology* (Wadsworth); *Massachusetts Review*; *Minnesota Poetry Anthology — 1973* (St. Cloud State U.); *New Letters*; *New Voices in American Poetry* (Winthrop); *New York Times*; *Nimrod*; *Open Places*; *Paris Review*; *Poems One Line & Longer* (Grossman); *Poetry* ("The Rowboat" copyright 1974 by the Modern Poetry Association); *Poetry Northwest*; *Prairie Schooner*; *Shenandoah*; *Southern Humanities Review*; *Southern Poetry Review*; *Three Rivers Poetry Journal*; *25 Minnesota Poets II* (Nodin Press); *University of Tampa Poetry Review*; *Westigan Review*; *Wisconsin Review*; *Wormwood Review*; *Yankee*.

"The Operation" copyright 1975 by *The Paris Review*, Inc. "The Women" first appeared in *California Quarterly*. Copyright © 1972 by The Regents of the University of California. "Rondel" copyright © 1976 by the National Council of Teachers of English. Reprinted by permission. "The Animals' Christmas" copyright 1970 by the New York Times Company. Reprinted by permission. "Porno Love" and "The Obscene Caller" reprinted from *The Massachusetts Review*, © 1975, The Massachusetts Review, Inc. "Jack, Afterwards" first appeared in *Prairie Schooner*, copyright © 1976 by the University of Nebraska Press. "The Rowboat" first appeared in *Poetry*. "Looking at Models in the Sears Catalogue" from *Heartland II: Poets of the Midwest*, copyright © 1975 by Northern Illinois University Press, DeKalb. Reprinted by permission of the publisher.

The author would also gratefully like to acknowledge receipt of the 1968 Yankee Poetry Award (First Prize) for "Storm," the 1974 Borestone Mountain Poetry Award (First Prize) for "The Birthday," a 1974 Discovery Award from the New York YM-YWHA's Poetry Center for a number of these poems, and three grants that helped with the completion of this book: a Southwest State University (Minnesota) faculty stipend, a National Endowment for the Arts Fellowship in Creative Writing, and a Minnesota State Arts Council Fellowship.

CONTENTS

III. THE CHERRY-TREE IS DOWN,
      AND DEAD

IV. SHE STANDS BETWEEN THE
      CANVAS AND THE CANDLE

I. SMILE A BEAST-SMILE

THE RISE AND FALL

The rise and fall
at the chest
of an animal.
There is patience
buried near some bellows

begun with time.
A continuing, precisely
right rhythm.
Thought has never
known such slow

steps:
the dance inside
caves of bone,
inhuman
repetitions

of love.
Still they move
with such surpassing
violence,
and explain

nothing.
Translate them!
Translate
the raised hoof.
Read me their story.

THE CAT

He has a history
of long, silent
descending
from trees.
He lands

years later
in the laps of women.
He brings with him
a memory
of waiting deep in leaves,

of bright claws he now
is amazed to find
grown short and tucked
like pale fingers
into the folds of a dress.

He has fallen
out of a life.
He tries to remember
a lake in a clearing,
but each time he would drink

from that memory
he discovers
in a blue saucer of milk
his face like a head
served up on a plate.

STORM

Fish at the hole
Cut wide in ice
Seem to shiver, stunned
At the sight of snow.

The water loses it
Immediately
But there is no end
To the soft flood.

The fish dive
In disbelief, return
And find it true,
The flakes growing even

Larger, filling
Their unblinking eyes.
Slowly their mouths
Open and shut,

Breathing nothing
Translatable about
This whiteness broken
So beautifully in air.

THE ANIMALS' CHRISTMAS

They are always living
in Christmas.
Though they walk years
through a field
they can never step

out of the birth of a god.
In each dark brain
a star
sending light through their sinews
leads their hooves

forward from one miracle
to another,
the gleams
tipping grass
like the bright eyes

of uncountable millions
of babies
a field has borne.
When they rub a tree,
a secret myrrh

descends onto their backs.
They carry and offer it
without even trying.
From their nostrils
they breathe good news.

THE STEPS ANIMALS TAKE

The steps animals take
are over our
bodies.
The great
spiritual

bellies
passing over
us. They are a constant
roof leaving us
exposed.

Like massive
guardian angels,
dressed in flowing
garments of blood,
they step carefully;

not once have they
crushed a life.
With no sky but their
gleaming undersides, no walls
but their bright shanks,

we walk in the midst
of a herd, its violence
translated
into a precise
dance.

A LESSON IN SNARLING

Fix the eyes
on someone not
you, then bare
the teeth out of
self-love.

If you move, make
it deep in the
throat. Believe
you cannot
lose ground.

Once his face
begins to go
rigid, the features
he met you with
drain out,

smile a beast-
smile, the invisible
breaking out
at knowing this
place is yours.

COMING IN FROM BEHIND

This is how to do it:
place your front two legs
on the back of your mate;
spread your hind legs wide
for stability.

You see nothing
of her face.
Your head is higher than hers.
This way she can browse,
head swung low,

mouth deep in the earth.
So mounting,
head to the sun,
you would appear proud
were the position not foolish.

But that is how to do it:
awkwardly loving
what is in front of you.
And note how you advance
when she advances,

down on all fours,
belly brushing the grass,
taking you —
upright like a man —
with her.

THE FISH OF HIS WOMAN

They have followed her
for years. They are still
with her. In dreams.
In magazines, watching her.
Circling under floors.

Or she will start to speak
and they will come
rushing beautifully out,
like trout
over a falls.

She wants dishware
with fish fired
into them. She is always
showing them a thigh,
luring them on.

Ask her who, what,
they are, and she dives
openmouthed and innocent
away. But these
fish-stories circulate:

they have been known
to live years on
dry land; for counting
on sleepless nights,
they can leap over a life.

THE UNICORN

If I've been lucky to see it in later years
Floating across some landscape in a dream,
I've my sister to thank. She never spoke of it
After that first time, but that was enough.
I was dead asleep. She came into my room
And shook me awake, saying she'd seen it.
(I was five, she twelve: fifty or so years ago,
Yet still I see the face I woke startled to
Emphatic as a single figure on stage.)
Seen what? I asked her, sitting up afraid.
The unicorn! Her eyes shone. The unicorn!
She'd seen it below her window, by the pond —
As white and delicate, she said, as an egg.
(Mother and Father slept at the other end
Of the hall, where the house fronted the road;
Our rooms were in the back, above the garden.)
I must have looked bewildered; she went on.
She'd been awakened by a sound of tapping
That seemed outside the house, yet inside, too.
She got up, went to her window and opened it,
Hugging herself against the cool Spring air.
Leaning out, she cried aloud to see it:
Moon-drenched, single-horned, in slow ballet,
The unicorn moved below from window to window
Tapping on glass as if to be let in:
It lowered its head outside each room and set
Its great horn to rest against the panes, then
With unnatural touch lifted it and let it fall:
The sounds were notes the influence of the moon
Seemed to make visible, single silver coins
To purchase something yet to be disclosed.
When my sister cried out,

                         the unicorn stopped.
He looked up and saw her, his animal-eyes
And her girl-eyes meeting in that half-light.
I knew from what my sister said, from the way
She said it, that such meeting of eyes was a special
Kind of knowing, a knowing both were meant for
And I should witness. He looked up, she down:

17

The air between them was a stairs, and what
Bright traffickings, could we have seen!
                                        Then he
Whirled backwards, all silent, and stepped or glided
(My sister said his moves were never clearly
This or that, but mixes of all moves)
Over to the old stone-encircled pond,
From which the fish had gone. Now it became
A center for him, a dark hub to hold him
In, as he did what he came for, or what
My sister thought he came for. What he did
Was dance. The garden was his stage. The pond
What he wove his moves, and himself, around.
It was a dance in ankle-deep moonlight,
Moonlight so thick upon the ground it seemed
The unicorn took care to move just so,
Fearing to displace the milky stuff.
He went round. He went round and made a world
Unto himself. He wove bright circles that night,
Circles within circles, and circles counter.
Where he went, weaving, the moonlight went,
Clung to his back like a load, a light performer.
And the horn, the starward horn, was as a rod,
Something straight to chastise all that roundness.
It divided the white air like a knife
Pulling through silk, but here the magic moonsilk
Healed itself behind the pulling blade.
If dance has tone as words and music do,
The tone of this dance flirted, yes and no;
Now sweet, a sliding through a fey medium,
Now muscled press against heavy air.
Nor did it change back and forth but was
Two in one, a simple melody spread
Into boughs, a skater on mirror-ice.
What was this dance so North *and* South?
Was it a wildness trimmed with ceremony
Or a ceremony rouged with wildness?
It seemed a measure formal yet hot, a kind
Of formal fire.

My sister told all this
In broken glimpses, pictures vague and loose,
Impressions wavering like underwater leaves,
As if the dance had witched her into dream.
But one moment she remembered well:
The unicorn rose on two legs, like one of us,
And slow-spun himself around the pond,
Impossibly erect, his forehooves raised
In ambiguous elevation, a white gesture.
The gesture made a center for the garden;
It gathered the garden to itself, held it
As if to kiss it somehow into meaning:
The pond a center for the unicorn,
The unicorn a center for the garden,
My sister a dream-center for my night.
She said the dance seemed something meant for her
And her alone, like words whispered in an ear,
Yet seemed somehow equally impersonal,
An impulse sent blindly from out a void
And destined before morning to recede.
It was then, his hooves high in the air,
The unicorn opened his mouth as if to speak
Or sing. My sister never knew; no sound
Came. But he held his mouth open like that
All the while he moved through his rehearsal
Of zero, moonzero. He made a procession
Of himself, a procession in its own track,
Eating itself up, or renewing itself
Or both.
            Then it was I screamed. In my sleep.
My sister thought it was the unicorn:
His mouth was open, a voice was on the air.
Soon the illusion broke. She heard me cry
And turned, startled, only to turn back and see
The unicorn gone, the moonlawn shadowed
By the long shadow of a growing cloud.
My sister said she shivered then, either
From cold air or thinking on that image:
His mouth open, and dumb, my voice afloat

19

And bodiless, something looking for a home.
She said I seemed to cry out on its behalf
Or it drew out my cry, with open mouth.
Whichever, things coming together that way
Frightened her, and so she turned and ran
Into my room, waking me, her face on fire
With that cool fire the unicorn had burned
Across the night. It burns across me now
When I think of it. It burned across her then
And for years afterwards. She didn't say so
But she didn't have to: the moves that moonbeast
Signed with his body on the air that night,
Like some bright power signing all its names,
Had been a promise made for her to see,
A promise hard to keep, yet impossible
Not to. I mean, there will be such burning
Though the air seem cold.
                                        Anyway, she woke me
And that's where I began. No, I won't say
My sister told it to me just that way.
My years have done something to the story.
Nor will I say her girlyears had nothing
To do with the story in the first place.
She gave me seeds. Hard, white seeds. Gave them
In the middle of the night. I was the soil.
I'm still the soil. The story is flowers.
And the flowers are white, like something bled.
I think the moon draws the blood down like that,
Back into the roots of things, and they go white
Like the unicorn. Men faint under the moon.
My dreams have gotten whiter through the years.
I'll see the unicorn against that white
One day, or not see him, snow on snow.

II. AN AIR A WOUND SINGS

THE PERFECTIONIST

Peter Kubelka, an Austrian filmmaker, has been making films for eighteen years but his total works run less than forty minutes. *Schwechater*, a film it took two years to make, lasts one minute.

Nowhere around him
is anything broken,
he is that careful.
His wife sits perfectly
in a corner,

his children are never
wound up to breaking.
The breaths he produces
are tied in ribbons,
fit for gifts.

When he stretches with
sleepiness, his arms extend
inward, away from the china;
when he speaks to friends,
he scratches each word on a stone.

All his life he's been moving
in slow motion up a long
flight of stairs — one step a year.
Nightly, he dreams of
diving into water

and not splashing.
But the nightmare recurs:
he is sailing
in a mistake like a boat
toward the edge of the world.

23

THUMB

The odd, friendless boy raised by four aunts.

THE AMPUTEE

Look at me move
My one, good hand.
I will conjure with it.

I will make
Another hand, as powerful,
And take it for my own.

With that new hand,
I will make signs
In the air. Even I

Shall not understand them.

THE STRICKEN CHILD

Enter her foot
With the doctor who
Cuts through
To the bone, baring

To put right
The way the deep
White web
Hangs together.

Move with the light
As it sings on
The tracery of bone
And living wire,

And feel how
The miles of thin
Fingers inside
Could pull tight

The net so
Delicately spread
Through her twelfth-
Year body.

Then imagine her
Only space
Drawing shut
And you within

Witnessing how
Death and beauty
Flash there
Along thin tracks.

AFTER A FIFTEENTH-CENTURY MINIATURE SHOWING KING MARK STABBING TRISTAN IN THE PRESENCE OF YSOLT

King Mark is in the doorway,
his eyes
and Ysolt's
on Tristan
bleeding.

It is a small room
where the triangle plays.
The floor is checkered.
Everything tilts
at wrong angles

in just the right way.
Ysolt raises
one meek hand.
Her fingers
fit the room

perfectly.
Such a charming stabbing!
The violence here
opens no mouths
except the mouth

in Tristan's back.
The sweetness of this violence
will never cloy.
It is an air
a wound sings.

CHAIN LETTER

Enclosed you will find the names
of every woman you have ever loved
and never stopped loving.
Write a letter to each of them
telling them so. They will not believe it.
Send along a photograph of yourself
in which you cannot be found:
say, This is what it has come to.
Tell them to observe your handwriting,
how — surprising for a man your age —
it wanders erratically like
some river on an old, faded map.
Lastly, remind them of the desperation
of chain letters, how the man who
gives his heart to the mails
always fears it will be returned
stamped, "Sender non-existent."
With your letters to the women
enclose a long list of names,
each of them yours.
Tell them the names need only be
spoken aloud when they're alone
or, when they lie with their loves,
to themselves, softly.
That will preserve the chain.
For your part, if you break the chain,
women you meet will look at you
as if you were a package, ticking,
they had just received.
If you do not break the chain,
all the women you write to

will come to you in dreams,
as delicate as envelopes
that have never been used,
and as exciting, able
to go anywhere.
Remember — this chain letter is illegal.
If you inform the authorities,
we will have to tell them
there must be some mistake,
how we know you, and how your love
has always been the dead letter
boxes have gone rusty waiting for.

FORM REJECTION LETTER

We are sorry we cannot use the enclosed.
We are returning it to you.
We do not mean to imply anything by this.
We would prefer not to be pinned down about this matter.
But we are not keeping — cannot, will not keep —
    what you sent us.
We did receive it, though, and our returning it to you
    is a sign of that.
It was not that we minded your sending it to us
    unasked.
That is happening all the time, they
    come when we least expect them,
        when we forget we have needed or might yet need them,
    and we send them back.
We send this back.
It is not that we minded.
At another time, there is no telling. . .
But this time, it does not suit our present needs.

We wish to make it clear it was not easy receiving it.
It came so encumbered.
And we are busy here.
We did not feel
    we could take it on.
We know it would not have ended there.
It would have led to this, and that.
We know about these things.
It is why we are here.
We wait for it. We recognize it when it comes.
Regretfully, this form letter does not allow us to elaborate
    why we send it back.
It is not that we minded.

We hope this does not discourage you. But we would not
    want to encourage you falsely.
It requires delicate handling, at this end.
If we had offered it to you,

perhaps you would understand.
But, of course, we did not.
You cannot know what your offering it
    meant to us,
And we cannot tell you:
There is a form we must adhere to.
It is better for everyone that we use this form.

As to what you do in future,
    we hope we have given you signs,
    that you have read them,
    that you have not mis-read them.
We wish we could be more helpful.
But we are busy.
We are busy returning so much.
We cannot keep it.
It all comes so encumbered.
And there is no one here to help.
Our enterprise is a small one.
We are thinking of expanding.
We hope you will send something.

LOOKING AT MODELS
IN THE SEARS CATALOGUE

These are our immortals.
They stand around
and always look happy.
Some must do work,
they are dressed for it,
but stay meticulously
clean. Others
play forever,
at the beach, in backyards,
but never move
strenuously. Here
the light is such
there are no shadows.
If anyone gestures,
it is with an open
hand. And the smiles
that bloom everywhere
are permanent, always
in fashion.
   So
it is surprising to discover
children here,
who must have sprung
from the dark of some loins.
For the mild bodies
of these men and women
have learned to stay
dry and cool:
even the undressed
in bras and briefs
could be saying,
It was a wonderful dinner,
thank you so much.
     Yet,
season after season,
we shop here:

in Spring's pages,
no ripe abundance
overwhelms us;
in Winter's pages,
nothing is dying.
It is a kind of perfection.
We are not a people
who abide ugliness.
All the folds in the clothing
are neat folds,
nowhere to get lost.

THE WOMEN

They are taking off their clothes.
They are admiring each other's bodies.

They have never met before.
They are at ease with each other.

There are countless numbers in
what seems a ballroom.

Some move about, unhurried.
Some recline, on each other.

No one eats or sleeps.
They go on like this forever.

There is no furniture here,
spareness luxuriates,

nor doors in or out,
windows open onto everything.

Men cannot find this place.
Women at windows see them

far below, as in a valley,
fumbling with buttons,

trying to crawl
under the roots of trees.

WATER

1

The man drowning
has these thoughts:
I have hands, feet,
a torso to give,
but no one, nothing
seems to want them.
Not even the water,
which keeps pushing
me down in its thoughts.
If I could rise
just once to the tip
of the water's tongue,
I know it would be pleased
to speak me.

2

Going down,
it is not what you think
at all. This is a place
to live,
I am convincing myself.
Each strange shape
I see
I make into something
familiar.
A stone is a fist,
a weed is a finger
pointing the way.
Soon I shall make
tables and chairs
out of fish.
I shall find a woman

the next time I open
my eyes. We will send
babies
up to the surface
whenever we speak.

3

When you strike bottom,
you bounce up
slowly, then
settle down.
No one coming upon me
years from now
will imagine the treasure
in my breast.
I have deep holds,
and it is still
not too late
for me to hear
the rude sailors
singing in my skull.

THE VOICES

The voices came
when I was eight.
High, whiney voices
of men whose faces I imagined
were small and pinched.
They chattered fast:
I never understood a word.

They'd come unexpectedly
like a summer storm
and I'd cry and run
trembling to my mother.
She couldn't help.
My father said something
about too much reading.

Our family doctor
admitted it was strange
but said he knew the cure:
one teaspoonful
of warm glycerine
in each ear
to drown the men.

So it was done.
When the voices rose
out of the dark of my ear,
when the disembodied souls
swarmed my head
like Satanic gnats
out to get me,

I'd lie on my side,
tearful and afraid,
while my mother tilted
sweet glycerine
warmed at the stove

into the bell of my ear.
Something worked:

the voices slid
slowly beneath the syrup,
sounding betrayed,
like figures in a mist
waving goodbye.
When I was nine,
silence came to live in my ear.

It lives there now.
It lets me sleep.
But when I do I dream
of lost messages,
of bottles floating
to shore and breaking,
their notes escaping as fish

beautifully untranslatable.

THE OBSCENE CALLER

Years ago,
he began a long dial
of your number.
At the precise moment
he finishes dialing,
you will arrive home.
He will not sound
as you might expect.
For a moment
you will think it could be
your father.
Gentle and patient,
he will understand
the great distance
you have had to come.
You ask him who he is.
He tells you his name
is not in the phonebook.
He cannot be called
by the authorities.
So reassuring is he,
that when he asks you
to take off your clothes,
you do so.
He says, Look at yourself.
You do so.
When he begins telling you
the secrets of your life,
you will not be inclined
to hang up.
He will use
the most graphic terms.
Nothing he says

will shock you.
If he is doing anything
with his free hand,
you will know it is only
checking the next name
on the list.
Soon you begin
to breathe heavily.
It will be he
who hangs up first.

THE OPERATION

They take out all the parts marked X. You watch this in a mirror above the operating table. You never knew you had so many parts marked X. You ask the doctor what the X means. He says, "Negligible." You worry about this, how your insides are rapidly growing hollow, how a heap of yourself is accumulating in a white pan. A nurse says something about all this going to feed stray dogs. She means well, to comfort you, but you cannot help thinking of the old days, how you posed for pictures in magazines, modelling swimming trunks. You were rich then. The first sign of trouble came when a woman put her hand up inside you, up through the hole you did not know you had. She grimaced, as if she had discovered something damp and maggoty, something luridly and obscenely alive. When she removed her hand, you both saw how it had already begun to turn black. Now the doctor is staring down at you. His face is goggled like a pilot's. You are so light now, so unballasted, you have begun to fly.

LEARNING TO SWIM IN MID-LIFE

I say, Water,
be good.
I do not
give myself to you
easily.
For so many years
I have walked bent low,
hugging the earth,
afraid to fall off.
Now you look at me
like a young woman
making me forget a wife
and children.
Now you would have me
lift both feet
off the ground at once.

So I enter you
and you keep me up,
longer than I have
ever expected.
I am not drowning.
I am light.
For once it would be easy
to carry myself.
With no strain,
I could give myself
to others.
I would say, Here,
take me. It would be that simple.
I would be in my hand.
In you now,

I have lost so much
of my heavy self,
even in the driest time
I would float to the top.

I stroke
and stroke again.
I am moving
with pleasure.
I think of all the other
bodies of water
I panicked in,
a man out
of his element.
Here, in the middle of my life,
my hands are taking
what they need
to pull me forward.
I am wet
with your wetness.

THE RECOVERY

"It is only when people begin to laugh that sanity returns."
— Robert Moses

I thought it was distant thunder
but it was only me
beginning to laugh.

I began to stand.
My body
was telling jokes
on itself,
it was that strong.

I took out my heart
and looked at it.
It was titled
Best Humorous Stories of the Year.
I had written them all.

This was something new,
rib-tickling health.
For years
I had put my head on the block
for the executioner, me.
It was a serious business
I failed at in the neck of time;
don't axe me why.

Now I wear this funny hat,
my old life.
I even wear it to bed:
with it on, I'm twice-naked.

I balance now, a clown on a low wire.
I am saving myself to the last,
like a punchline.
My sanity is endless,
like the story of the shaggy dog.

I do not know how this happened.
I think that is funny.

JACK, AFTERWARDS

It's difficult to say what it all meant.
The whole experience, in memory,
Seems like a story someone might invent
Who was both mad and congenitally cheery.
I have to remind myself, it happened to me.
The stalk's gone now, and Alma, the old cow;
And I fear only the dream with the shadow.

My mother had a lot to do with it.
In fact, you might say it was her beanstalk —
She scattered the seeds, I didn't, when she hit
My full hand and said all I was good for was talk.
She haunted me in those days: I couldn't walk
Anywhere without seeing her face,
Even on the crone in the giant's palace.

Throughout this whole time, my father was dead.
I think I must have felt his not-being-there
More than I would have his being-there. Instead
Of his snoring, his absence was everywhere.
So the old man with the beans, poor and threadbare
As he was, became the more important
To my boyish needs. Not to mention the giant.

Oddly enough, the beanstalk itself, which some
Might think the most wonderful part of all this,
Pales in time's perspective. Though my true home
Between the earth and sky, and though no less
Than magic, that stalk, in the last analysis,
Was but a means to an end. Yet, I must say,
I still recall the beanflowers' sweet bouquet.

Then there's the giant. What can be said? Nothing
And everything. Or this: if the truth be known
About someone so great, it was surprising

How vulnerable he seemed, and how alone.
Not that I wasn't frightened. I was, to the bone —
But it was his weakness, joined to such power,
I feared most, and fear now, any late hour.

The fruits of it all were gold, a hen, and a harp.
I wish I could say I miss my poverty,
When my appetite, if not my wit, was sharp,
But I don't. A little fat hasn't hurt me
Much. Still it's that strange harp's melody,
Beauty willing itself, not golden eggs,
Whose loss would leave me, I hope, one who begs.

Of everything, the strangest was to see
Alma the cow come back home at the end,
Her two horns wreathed in wild briony
And traveler's joy. Did the old man send
Her as a gift? She seemed, somehow, lightened.
I'd like to think I traded her away
To get her back, sea-changed, in such array.

So I sit here, my dying, blind mother
To tend to, and wonder how it was
I escaped, smiling, from such an adventure.
If events in those days conformed to laws,
I'd like to know — not least, nor only, because
What happened then still makes me ask, Why me?
Not even my mother knew, when she could see.

SAWING A WOMAN
IN HALF

It is done like this:
you gain her confidence.
You tell her how
for years
you sawed yourself in half,

only to come together
day after day.
Tell her: though the cleaving
was never painless,
you came to love

the applause you earned
and that you gave yourself.
Admit it is no trick:
yes, you are open
to all winds;

you can easily see
inside yourself
below the waist.
Keep till last this comfort:
you lie down with her, too.

Only then tell her how
there is no telling
when the magician will appear,
or who it will be,
or if it is you, or she.

HOW I ESCAPED FROM THE LABYRINTH

It was easy.
I kept losing my way.

III. THE CHERRY-TREE
IS DOWN, AND DEAD

SMALL DARK SONG

The cherry-tree is down, and dead, that was so high,
And Wind, that did this thing, roams careless while you cry,
For Wind's been everywhere today, and has an alibi.

THE BLACK DEATH

There had been portents:
In Rome, blood poured
From freshly-cut bread;
A fiery column
Hung over Avignon;

And a great dog roamed
The German sky with a drawn
Sword in his paws —
An angel rode his back
And laughed. Then it struck:

Stately manors
And poor hovels
Emptied to fill
Each pit with a hundred
Shovelled dead.

The sure sign was this:
A swelling below
The shoulder, a bubo —
Known in the street
As "shilling in the armpit."

Doctors warned, Move
Slowly, if at all.
Sing but little.
When air comes in,
So does poison.

Men walked outside
With fragrant spices
Raised to their noses:
The perfume of death
Could take away breath.

Some shut all doors
And windows, ate
The most delicate fare.
Sweet music was played
And they listened hard.

Others went out
To meet it square
With a dying whore:
The lifted prick
Mocks the limp sick.

Children whispered how,
At night, one could see
Blue flames leap
Out of the mouths of the dead
And dance, ghostly, overhead,

And their parents couldn't
Keep from dreaming
All night of drinking
From a dying man
His thick, black urine.

So the flagellants
Marched, who whipped
Themselves with sticks
Until blood came
And the good death of orgasm.

But victims need victims:
The plague, all knew,
Was a hellish Jew-
Plot. Rabinowitz
Got a knife in the throat.

Everywhere, Death rushed
And Profit kept pace:
Men hawked dice
With the pips filled in
And prayers painted on:

Oremus. Our Father
Who art in heaven.
Seven and eleven.
Throw the bones. I pass.
Lord, have mercy on us.

RONDEL

A beautiful snow falls on a bed,
Amazing the man and woman there.
It falls between and over them where
Just before they lay close and naked.

They wonder if anything they said
Or did called down so cold through the air
This beautiful snow onto their bed
To amaze any who would love there;

They wonder if snowmen can be wed,
And if white is what they'll always wear,
And if lovers should sing or shiver
As they watch fall the uninvited
And beautiful snow onto their bed.

THE ROWBOAT

The rowboat seems to call
To me tonight. I hear small lake-waves slap
   And rock it like a cradle
On the dark shore below the house, where sleep

Refuses to come to my bed.
The house is empty of my wife and children,
   Who are gone, she said, for good
This time. And so the rowboat says, Come down.

I take for my nakedness
A blanket draped around my shoulders and go
   Down through the grove of trees
To where the boat's all alive in shadow:

It seems to me a hand
Beckoning, sticking out of the lake's sleeve,
   Or now a deep lap spread
Wide like a mother's, and I her suckling love.

I push off, one bare foot
Dry and secure in the boat's dipping bow,
   The other shocked by the wet
Cold swirl. It's an awkward way, the only I know.

The small boat eases out,
As if it belonged here, and sits upon
   The lake's top like the right-
Ful and resolute heir to the night's throne.

What am I doing here,
The artifice of a blanket thinly disguising
   How poor I am, and an oar
In each hand poised as for a purpose? Something

Turns the boat around.
The wind has picked up, wants to take the boat
   And me its own way. "Wind,
Is this why I've come here in the dark? To sit

And ponder what you mean?
And, that known, whether you mean good or ill?

Whether I should cut clean
Against the pushing waves, against your will,

   By striking so, like this,
Making spray fly, the rowboat dive and lift,
   Or whether I should kiss
Your great face tenderly and learn to drift?"

   Whatever the wind knows,
It only blows and blows. The pine trees bend
   And bend before such force,
Like saints for whom kneel is a prelude to stand.

   But I am no saint. If
I let go or battle, I am no sainted hero.
   I am the man in rough
Water who could drown in all he doesn't know.

   A loon's call! It's so near
It startles me. I search the dark and see,
   Skimming across the water
And making a great fuss, a male loon up to

   His old tricks: three other loons,
A female and two chicks, are swimming the other way,
   And the protective father means
To distract me. I let myself be led astray.

   I see the house beyond
The trees and stroke and stroke again to get there.
   That's the decision: the wind
Won't push me where it will. I'll go counter.

   Yet I know that solves nothing.
Direction, says the loon, can be misdirection:
   I think of me moving
One way upon this lake, my wife and children

   Moving another way
Upon some road, and I know I can't say who's
   Going where, or why.
I only say: I row, and believe I choose.

SHE TELLS HIM WHY SHE LIKES MEN IN UNIFORM

I am not in love with war
Or blood or death or foolish men's
Ideas of honor, that
"Mere scutcheon" — stupidity
Is stupidity, dressed up or not.

But I am in love
With covering our poor flesh
In costumes claiming for us
Something more, perhaps, than we deserve,
A certain style, a grandness.

It is our mortality
We drape. And let it be
Not only with uniforms
But long, beaded gowns,
Bright boots, or hats with wide brims.

The starred suit of the magician says,
"This man surpasses man;
This man makes gold from base stuff."
It is a lovely lie, and good:
We do not want the woman sawn in half.

Ours is no age for ladies
Distressed or not,
And you, my lord, are no lord.
But let us play like children
With old clothes, and pretend.

I hear the form in uniform:

Such dressing up is civilized,
Though armies kill.
It is equivalent to what the heartsick
Gentleman wears, a smile.

There goes a soldier
And my heart beats fast.
How handsome he looks, and noble!
Do not remind me I shall die tomorrow,
Nor tell me love is impossible.

IV. SHE STANDS BETWEEN THE CANVAS AND THE CANDLE

INSTRUCTIONS TOWARD
A NUDE

Start with the feet, where she touches the ground.
   It is important how
You shape them: from the feet everything else
   Will follow: she stands or falls
According to the way they meet the low
   Earth in its tilt and roll
Around the sun. Work up from there. The legs
   Look better if they bend
Even a little, as if absorbing
   Some quick shock or lifelong
Tremor from a depth past hope of measure.
   Then come the thighs. Be more
Than generous with these. They bear the weight
   Of infants, lovers, what
Do they not bear? Let them be wide and full.
   You are halfway now; still
You are just beginning. Where there are the crack
   And beard, let it be dark,
Dark. (Great tact is needed here in your sketch.
   Do not fill in too much.)
Then the belly. Think of a fruit's contour.
   One stroke and you have her
Pregnant. Above the ripening belly hang
   The breasts. There is nothing
To say for guidance here except a child
   Will suck from these. The world
Is round; let the child's first loves be round, too.
   (Beneath one beats what you
Cannot see or draw. This, which is not there,
   Gives life to your picture
Or it has none.) The arms make a gesture
   Forward, to the viewer:
Perhaps they invite; perhaps they offer him
   What is not shown in the hands.
The neck is a bridge — a mere transition
   Tapered and flushed and fine —
To the head. Here is trouble. The wise artist
   Brought up on the classic

Will not try to render the individual
   Face, the sole, brainy soul
Peering out of the eyes. Let her be all
   Women, the beautiful
General. Concentrate instead on the hair.
   Men have gotten lost here.
If it sweeps up high, it will lead the eye
   To heaven. Only you
Can decide if that is the best direction
   To go. Hair falling down
Over the shoulders leads you back to where
   You started from. Whichever
Way you choose, the whole effect should be of one
   Who feels herself at home
In that flesh. Success might be yours if you do
   It with love, and let it show.

PORNO LOVE

For Darlene & Mae

You send me a photograph
of you in which your genitals
are not only exposed
but offered close-up to the lens
like a piece of good advice.
I've never met you
though you say,
"We think you're swell."
I appreciate the gesture:
I've been exposing my genitals
in poems for a long time now,
at least when they're good.
So I know you mean nothing obscene
by it. Your squat is humble,
as mine is, even now.
I am writing this poem
naked, up close.
I am writing it with my penis.
No one but you two sisters
will understand
how such a poem is innocent,
how, as with a confidence to a friend,
no shock is intended,
how what we stick in the faces of our loved ones
is our way of saying, I trust you will not
seal me shut
or cut me off, I love you that much.
Surely we will meet with our clothes on,
that is the point.
But when I say, Thanks for the picture, Girls,
it's nicely cropped,
and you say, We liked the feel of your poem,
I'll be thinking how certain private parts
made vulnerable
give greatest pleasure
in a consummation
of good will.

THE RING POEM: A HUSBAND LOSES HIS WEDDING BAND AS HE GESTURES FROM A BRIDGE

It was an accident, and accidents
Don't mean, of course, but still the wedding ring
Flew off my finger, down into the river.
It was so hard and small it fell all full
Of direction, not the way paper does,
Seemingly unsure it wants to fall,
But like a stone that knows its place is down
And down. Shocked, you and I could only watch.
Age thins my fingers, and the air was cold:
I'd meant to tape the ring that very morning
but there it was, on its own, a hurtling child.

The time it took falling was a mere flash;
In memory it seems a slow descent.
I see it now, all camera-slowed, lovely
Arc, fine fragment of what circle, and now
-stopped: see, a bead of shining, knot of light.
But let it fall. There, already it breaks
The water, like a baby, coming through.
In my end is my beginning and
So forth. We know all that. This was a ring,
Hard and cold, falling into water, no
More and no less. It wasn't any fish
That sucks now at bottom on river muck,
It wasn't any angel with clipped wings.

It was a ring, a wheel, a wife, a life,
It wasn't anything I understand,
It was a silver thing to catch for prize,
It told unbrokenness, and other lies,
Was silent, always, didn't say a word.
But you did. With your darkening eyes, said this:
"Was that I? I felt a fluttering here
In my being's center, as if I fell.
I've felt it before. It comes over me

Sometimes when I'm on the solidest ground —
A sense of gravity, and I am grave.
I've been falling for years. I'll keep falling,
No one can catch me. I think you fall with me
And that we shine in falling, like your ring."
The brown river snaked away under us.
It took the ring, and tried to take our faces,
But our faces held, dancing on the surface.
I took your hand, meaning to say by touch:
"What it was I lost just now, I don't know.
I expect never to know for certain.
But, in going away, whatever it was
Curved as if, given enough time and space,
It would return. Perhaps it will come back
Transformed beyond recognition, some new
Round thing bending the lines of our lives to it.
It shall be a kind of good encirclement."
Suddenly I felt my finger's nakedness.
I clasped, unclasped, then pocketed my hands.
If you noticed, you didn't give any sign —
Except you picked up small stones from the bridge
And seeded the water with them, making rings.

THE BIRTHDAY

Thirty candles and one
to grow on. My husband
and son watch me
think of wishes.

I wish I found it
easier to make wishes
than I do. Wasn't it,
years ago, easy to make wishes?

My husband and son *are* wishes.
It is as if
every day I wait for them
to happen again,

and they do.
But surely there is much
I am without, yet
I stand here, wishless.

Perhaps I want
what I needn't wish for,
my life: it is
coming, everything will happen.

Or perhaps I want
precisely what I don't know,
all that darkness
so tall and handsome before me.

I have seen women age
beautifully, with a
growing, luminous
sexuality:

now I know, each year
they've been slowly
stepping out of their wishes
like their clothes.

I stand here amazed
at what is happening to me,
how I've begun to lighten
of desires, getting down

to my secret skin,
the impossibly thin
membrane this side
of nothing. Husband,

I wish I could tell you.

THE BED

1

Tonight the bed seems to float.
We are not in it,
are miles away,
but in the imagination it grows larger
and more luminous than it has seemed
all these years.

What it floats on
is not clear,
whether it be real water in a dream
or something we did
heavier than the bed itself,
too much to displace,
or the dark hand of sleep,
one of the flowers of an immense
eternal body.

But that it floats
is clear from the heave
beneath it that it rides.
It is not still
the way it would be
sunken to some bottom.

2

To say the bed is a ship
shrouded in mist,
its crew,
if it has a crew,
visible at the rail
only as dark, rocking smears

or to say it lies
open on a bright sea,
a clipper with precise
and light-edged lines
moving fast

is to trade one mask
for another, and in each case
to arouse the well-known
paradox, that the masked
is both hidden
and revealed by the mask.

And the masks are cheap.
The bed itself is a subtler entity,
tangible
but elusive
like music,
notes floating on air,
with a meaning
the body knows best.

3

Swimmers burst upon the mind
as into water,
two of them,
their bodies sexless,
wet and gleaming
though distant
and easily lost
among the surf and breakers.

They emerge dripping
upon a kind of floating
deck, raised on pontoons,
far out from shore.

It is not certain whether
they are like sleepers
emerging from a dream
to waken in bed

or like watchers
exhausted and climbing
into bed to sleep,

69

but the beauty
of the artificiality
of the flat
square-cornered
platform
amidst the ceaseless
and dangerous
roil

is certain.

4

A painter by candlelight
paints a fantasy of a bed.
A bed like a ship in a harbor,
about to set out.

The painter's wife enters the room,
.her long hair wet
and alive with small sea-life.
Her husband paints with a fish.

While he works on the details —
the bells in the tower of the church above the harbor,
the promising outlines on the horizon,
the texture of the water —
she stands between the canvas and the candle
and casts her shadow on the forming scene.

They wait for that moment
when they shall leave the room
and enter the picture,
when its parts coalesce,

when something in the painting
barely but discernibly
moves,

a small boy on the dock
begins to hurl a stone

or the ship itself,
looking oddly spiritual
in the sun,
shivers
at the engines' first
faint tremblings,
at the promise
of the flung stone.

A SURREALISTIC PHOTOGRAPH BY MANUEL ALVAREZ BRAVO (1938)

It is purely visual and tactile.
A naked girl
lies on her back by an adobe wall,
the sun directly overhead and full

so that her underside is all
shadow
and her topside glares so
as to make her body two

halves, what we know
and don't know. They are
one. She sleeps here forever,
one arm under

her head, the other
at her bush, easy.
Then these, strangely:
a barbed cactus ear laid nearby

and white bandages around thigh
and ankle. Is she sacrifice?
She lies
with one knee raised

on a blanket that could be an altar.
I love her.
I am the dust falling through the air.
I am landing now on lip, nipple, and hair.

TO ARIADNE:
A THANK YOU LETTER

Thank you for the thread. It worked
just fine. I don't know what I did
to deserve it. It was such a surprise,
coming like that in the mail,
wrapped in the plainest brown paper,
my name and town printed
in what seemed a child's hand,
no name or return address in the corner —
how confident you must have been
I would get it! —
    and, inside,
that bright ball of red thread
the free end of which was attached
to a gift-card saying simply, "Love, Ariadne."

I do not want to sound
ungrateful. I am grateful.
But you forgot to tell me the thread
could not be re-used. Recent events
have proven the old thread
has a tendency to break. In places
it has frayed away to practically

nothing. And the color does not stay:
it is as washed-out as the cheek
of someone who has forgotten
there are always good reasons to blush.

Don't misunderstand me: I am not asking
for another thread. Surely one
is more than my quota.
      I only want to say
I am taking up sewing. Believe me,
I do not mean to joke. Soon I shall be surrounded
by thread. Spool upon spool. My house
will be full of it. And then,
the next time I notice my life

is turning and twisting, and that the light is bad,
Ariadne, to prove how much I love you
I will burn down that house
without regret. And I will expect nothing
in the mail. A bill, the usual junk,
a solicitation for money, for love —
I shall receive all with the same smile,
I shall be happy to get anything. Ariadne,
because I love you, I can even be content
with an empty mailbox, a cold wind
and this old coat that has started unraveling.

EDWARD WESTON
IN MEXICO CITY

Clouds, torsos, shells, peppers, trees, rocks, smokestacks.
Let neither light nor shadow impose on these things
To give them a spurious brilliance or romance,
Let the mystery be the thing itself revealed
There for us to see better than we knew we could.
The pepper. The simple green pepper. Not so simple.
There are no two alike. Sonya brings me new peppers
Every day and each one leads me to the absolute
In its own way. My friends tell me the peppers
I've done cause physical pain and make
Beads of sweat pop out on the forehead. Orozco,
As soon as he saw them, said they were erotic.
I know nothing of that. I only know
Or seek to know the inner reality
Of each particular fruit, the secret
It tries but fails to hide because
In truth it would be known and taken;
The secret is of itself and beyond itself.
This pepper here: follow its form
And you enter an abstract world,
Yet always what you are making love to
Is pepper, pepper, pepper. It can both be
And not be itself.
                    The naked female body
When looked at in the right, that is the askew, way
Can also disappear while remaining fully
Present. Yesterday Tina was lying naked on the azotea
Taking a sun-bath. I was photographing clouds.
Then I noticed her and came down to earth
To shoot three dozen negatives in twenty minutes.
It was Tina I took, yet, in this picture,
Her right hip rises to become a slope
On the other side of Nature, and the ribs

The ribs are hesitancies, a fineness that will go
Only so far amidst the mass then wait
To be discovered by the quiet ones.
Tina, hello and goodbye, and hello.

Just don't ask me to make a formula of this.
With a formula I'd catch only the appearance
Of a secret. But I must disappoint my friends
By always starting over again, day after day,
So that they say, "That's not a Weston, take it out!"
When the sun rises, I become ignorant again,
Unburdened of yesterday's victories. Today
It has been shells. Two shells, one a
Chambered Nautilus. I balanced them together,
One inside the other. White background, black background.
I even tried my rubber raincoat for a ground.
The shells would slip near to breaking.
I am near to breaking, too. That is my formula.
No, I break. I lose myself in the shells.
My friends are right, it's not a Weston, I'm gone,
Thank God. Gone into the luminous coils.
A coil's urge is to become a circle;
I'm what the coil needs to close the gap.
Pepper, torso, shell: they're circle, circle, circle.

And now for sleep. I'm going to look at the dark.
When I wake up, I won't know what I've seen
But I'll have seen it nevertheless. Tomorrow
I'll look at what's under the sun; if I see right,
I'll be remembering what I see tonight.

CARNEGIE-MELLON POETRY

The Living and the Dead, Ann Hayes (1975)

In the Face of Descent, T. Alan Broughton (1975)

The Week the Dirigible Came, Jay Meek (1976)

Full of Lust and Good Usage, Stephen Dunn (1976)

*How I Escaped from the Labyrinth
          and Other Poems,* Philip Dacey (1977)

The Lady from the Dark Green Hills, Jim Hall (1977)

Books in the Carnegie-Mellon University Press Poetry Series are
distributed by the University of Pittsburgh Press, 127 N. Bellefield
Avenue, Pittsburgh, Pennsylvania 15260